Grade 2 Piano

CW00666417

Improve your scales!

Paul Harris

This book contains scale preparation in a selection of keys that support multiple exam boards including the ABRSM, Trinity College, LCM and MTB. Tick the keys you need to learn for your exam below.

Introduction

Scales, arpeggios and broken chords are important. And if taught and learned imaginatively, they can be fun!

Improve your scales! is designed to help you approach scale learning methodically and thoughtfully. Its intention is to turn learning scales into a pleasant, positive and relevant experience by gradually building up the skills to play them through cumulative and enjoyable activities.

What *Improve your scales!* is about
The idea of *Improve your scales!* is to present you with lots of engaging activities that lead up to playing the scale (and arpeggio or broken chord). Actually playing the scale is the last thing you do! These activities build up an understanding (of the fingering, technical issues, the sound, particular features, sense of key and connections with the pieces that you play) to help make the learning of scales really relevant.

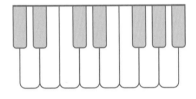

At the top of each scale is a keyboard showing the notes of that particular scale (the minor keys have two keyboards for the harmonic and melodic minor patterns). This is for you to fill in with whatever you find most useful. Here are some suggestions:
- highlight or colour in the notes of the scale – so you can see the pattern of black and white notes.
- fill in the note names.
- add the fingering you will use for both hands.

Here are two really important **Golden Rules:**

No 1 Before practising your scales make sure that you:
- Drink some water (this helps get the brain working!)
- Relax (especially shoulders, arms, wrists and fingers)
- Check your posture.

No 2 Always practise the scale and arpeggio or broken chord of the pieces you are learning.

How to use this book
This book contains all the scales you need to support ABRSM, Trinity, LCM and MTB Grade 2 exams. There is a complete list of all of the relevant scales, arpeggios and broken chords written out at the back of the book for you to refer to; with a teacher, tick those scales you need to learn for your exam, and whether you are required to play hands separately or hands together.

Acknowledgements
With great thanks to Lynn Arnold, Andrew Eales and Emily Bevington.

Scale patterns made easy!

There are actually only a few different fingering patterns used for scales. Once you have these clearly in your mind you'll see that fingering scales is really easy to master!

Every basic scale (major or minor) has eight notes – but we only have five fingers. So we have to devise simple repeated patterns that will allow us to play the scales comfortably and fluently. Once you understand the pattern you've virtually learnt to play the scale!

The most common pattern for the two-octave range scales in Grade 2 (**Pattern A**) is:

RH 123 **1**234 **1**23 **1**2345
LH 54321 **3**21 **4**321 **3**21

The **exception** for Grade 2 is F major right hand and B minor left hand (**Pattern B**). This is because there is a black key for the 4th note (on the way up in F major and on the way down in B minor), so we can't put our thumb on it! So we simply start the pattern with a group of 4 notes:

F major RH 1234 **1**23 **1**234 **1**234
B minor LH 4321 **4**321 **3**21 **4**321

There is a new pattern to learn for Grade 2 – B♭ major. This is because the scale begins on a black key. For comfort and ease, thumbs are rarely used on black keys in scales, so we use the following pattern (which we'll call **Pattern C**):

B♭ major RH 2 123 **1**234 **1**23 **1**234
B♭ major LH 321 **4**321 **3**21 **4**321 **2**

Arpeggios

Most of the Grade 2 arpeggios use the same pattern:

RH 123 1235
LH 5321 321 or 5421 421 (choosing which is most comfortable)

The exception is B♭ major (as it starts on a black note):
B♭ major RH 2 124 124
B♭ major LH 321 321 2 or 421 421 2

Broken chords

In broken chords we use fingers 1 and 5 in each group but the middle note varies between 3 and 2 – can you spot why it alters?

A scale a day!

Scales are both useful and fun. They're not like medicine – to be taken when you're not feeling well! Many patterns in your pieces are based on scales, so knowing them can be a real shortcut in learning pieces.

Try practising your scales with *character* – it makes them much more interesting to play. Practise one a day choosing from these characters and make up more of your own:

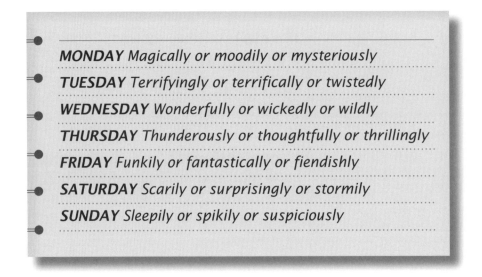

MONDAY *Magically or moodily or mysteriously*

TUESDAY *Terrifyingly or terrifically or twistedly*

WEDNESDAY *Wonderfully or wickedly or wildly*

THURSDAY *Thunderously or thoughtfully or thrillingly*

FRIDAY *Funkily or fantastically or fiendishly*

SATURDAY *Scarily or surprisingly or stormily*

SUNDAY *Sleepily or spikily or suspiciously*

Also, don't come down the way you went up!
Here are some ideas:

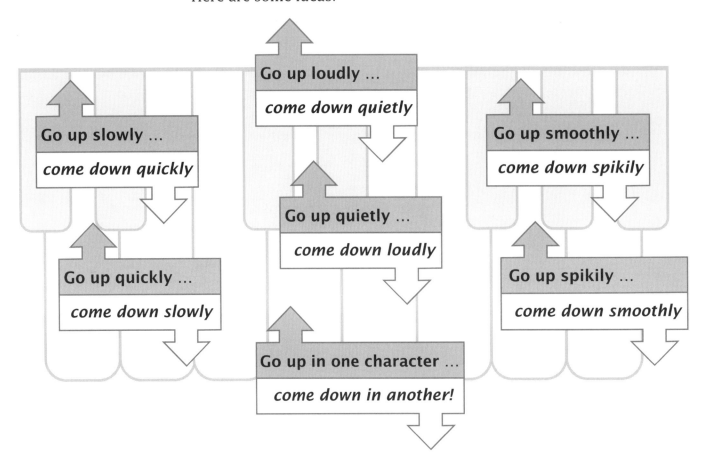

Go up loudly …
come down quietly

Go up slowly …
come down quickly

Go up quietly …
come down loudly

Go up smoothly …
come down spikily

Go up quickly …
come down slowly

Go up spikily …
come down smoothly

Go up in one character …
come down in another!

Why are scales important?

There are many reasons and it's important that you know them!

Tick if you agree:

- ☐ Scales will hugely improve all aspects of your finger technique, facility and control.
- ☐ Arpeggios and broken chords will improve your ability to move around the piano with ease.
- ☐ Knowing your scales and arpeggios will speed up the learning of new pieces because so much material is based on scale and arpeggio patterns.
- ☐ Knowing your scales and arpeggios will improve your sight-reading both in dealing with technical issues and reading melodic patterns.
- ☐ Knowing your scales and arpeggios will develop your sense of key.
- ☐ Playing scales and arpeggios or broken chords well and with confidence will earn good marks in exams.

Scales and exams

So that's why scales are an important part of exams! They really do help to develop your playing.

In an exam, the examiner will be listening out for:

- ☐ Evenness of pulse and rhythm
- ☐ Control and evenness of tone
- ☐ No unnecessary accents
- ☐ A sense of key
- ☐ The smooth passage of the thumb
- ☐ Fluency and dexterity
- ☐ A musical shape for each example

Think about each of these during practice sessions. Tick each off when you feel you have achieved them.

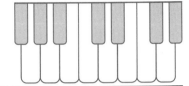

G major

Fill in the scale:
(See page 2 for details of how to do this)

Write the key signature of G major (treble and bass clefs): ══════════   ══════════

The relative minor of G major is: _____

TOP TIP *Practise each repeated section separately first, then play the whole exercise repeating until you are confident and fluent.*

Finger fitness

Broken chord exercises

Note: There is no G major arpeggio required for any Grade 2 exam.

1

Key piece Graceful goblins

2

Have a go Using both hands, or just the right-hand line, compose or improvise an answering phrase or a short piece beginning with these notes:

3

Sight-reading

1 In which key is this piece?

2 Can you spot any repeated patterns?

3 What will you count? Tap the rhythm of each line separately, then both lines together.

4 How will you bring character to your performance?

5 Try to hear the music in your head before you begin.

4

You are now ready to **say** the notes, **hear** the scale or broken chord in your head (playing the keynote first), **think** about the fingering and then finally **play** the scale or broken chord with confidence!

D major

Fill in the scale:

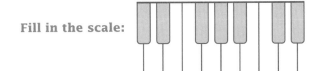

Write the key signature of D major (treble and bass clefs):

The relative minor of D major is: _____

TOP TIP *Practise the Finger fitness exercises hands separately or hands together depending on your exam requirements.*

Finger fitness

Arpeggio exercises

Note: There is no D major broken chord required for any Grade 2 exam.

1

Key piece   Daring dolphin

2

Have a go Using both hands, or just the right-hand line, compose or improvise an answering phrase or a short piece beginning with these notes:

3

Sight-reading

1 In which key is this piece?

2 Which notes are affected by the key signature?

3 What will you count? Tap the rhythm of each line separately, then both lines together.

4 How will you bring character to your performance?

5 Try to hear the music in your head before you begin.

See also *Improve your sight-reading!* Piano Grade 2, Stage 3: D major.

4

You are now ready to **say** the notes, **hear** the scale or arpeggio in your head (playing the keynote first), **think** about the fingering and then finally **play** the scale or arpeggio with confidence!

A major

 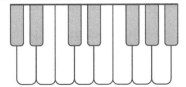

Write the key signature of A major (treble and bass clefs):

The relative minor of A major is: _____

Finger fitness

TOP TIP *Make sure you control the speed and rhythm when you change direction.*

Right-hand exercises

1

2

3

Left-hand exercises

4

5

6

Arpeggio exercises

7

8

Note: There is no A major broken chord required for any Grade 2 exam.

1

Key piece   Aimless afternoons

2

Have a go Using both hands, or just the right-hand notes, compose or improvise an answering phrase or a short piece beginning with these notes:

3

Sight-reading

1 What is the key of this piece?

2 What pattern is formed by the left-hand notes in bars 1 and 2?

3 What is the first note in the right hand called?

4 Find the G sharps. (*Clue: there are only two!*)

5 Tap the rhythm of each hand separately and then both hands together.

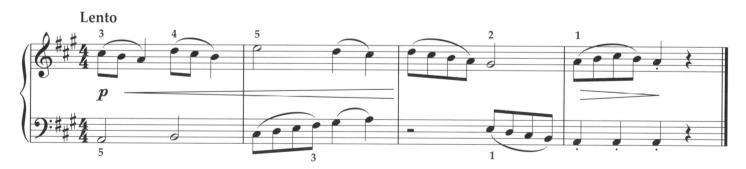

4

You are now ready to **say** the notes, **hear** the scale or arpeggio in your head (playing the keynote first), **think** about the fingering and then finally **play** the scale or arpeggio with confidence!

E major

Fill in the scale:

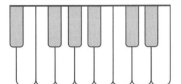

Write the key signature of E major (treble and bass clefs):

The relative minor of E major is: _____

> **TOP TIP** *When practising your scales avoid accenting the top note, or landing on the last note with a bump.*

Finger fitness

Arpeggio exercises

Note: There is no E major arpeggio or broken chord required for any Grade 2 exam.

Key piece Etude

Have a go Using both hands, or just the right-hand line, compose or improvise an answering phrase or a short piece beginning with these notes:

Sight-reading

1 In which key is this piece?
2 What is the name of the second note in the right hand?
3 How many times does the slurred left-hand pattern in bar 1 appear?
4 How many G sharps can you spot in this piece?
5 Tap the rhythm of each hand separately, then both hands together.

You are now ready to **say** the notes, **hear** the scale in your head (playing the keynote first), **think** about the fingering and then finally **play** the scale with confidence!

The complete scale and broken chord are given on pages 35 and 40

F major

Fill in the scale:

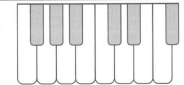

Write the key signature of F major (treble and bass clefs):

The relative minor of F major is: _____

> **TOP TIP** *Remember, F major uses a different pattern in the right hand (**Pattern B**).*

Finger fitness

Broken chord exercises

Note: There is no F major arpeggio required for any Grade 2 exam.

1

Key piece   Frolic

2

Have a go Using both hands, or just the right-hand line, compose or improvise an answering phrase or a short piece beginning with these notes:

3

Sight-reading

1 In which key is this piece?

2 Can you spot any scale patterns?

3 What will you count? Tap the rhythm of each line separately, then both lines together.

4 How will you bring character to your performance?

5 Try to hear the music in your head before you begin.

4

You are now ready to **say** the notes, **hear** the scale or broken chord in your head (playing the keynote first), **think** about the fingering and then finally **play** the scale or broken chord with confidence!

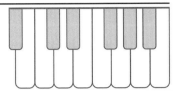

B♭ major

Fill in the scale:

Write the key signature of B♭ major (treble and bass clefs): _____ _____

The relative minor of B♭ major is: _____

> **TOP TIP** *Remember, this key uses a new finger pattern in both hands (**Pattern C**).*

Finger fitness

Arpeggio exercises

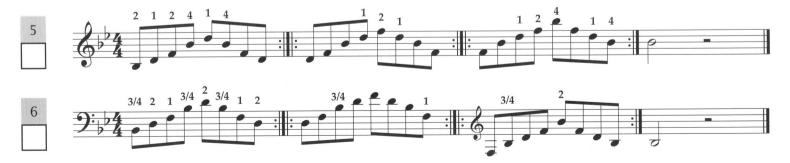

Note: There is no B♭ major broken chord required for any Grade 2 exam.

Key piece **Blueberries**

Have a go Using the left-hand line given, compose or improvise an answering phrase or a short piece for the left hand or hands together:

Sight-reading

1 In which key is this piece?

2 Which notes are flattened?

3 Can you find the E flat?

4 Tap the pulse and hear the upper part in your head.

5 This piece has a calm character – how will you bring this out in your performance?

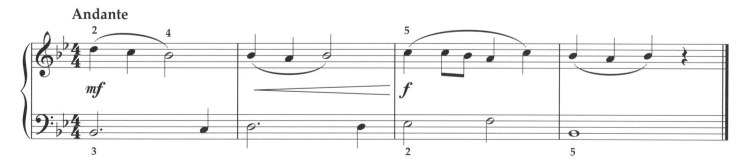

You are now ready to **say** the notes, **hear** the scale or arpeggio in your head (playing the keynote first), **think** about the fingering and then finally **play** the scale or arpeggio with confidence!

A minor

Fill in the scale:
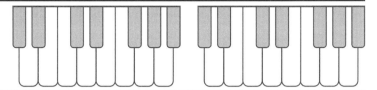

Write the key signature of A minor (treble and bass clefs): _____
Perhaps this is a trick question!

The relative major of A minor is: _____

Finger fitness

Harmonic minor exercises

If you play G instead of G♯, you get the **natural minor** scale.

Arpeggio exercises

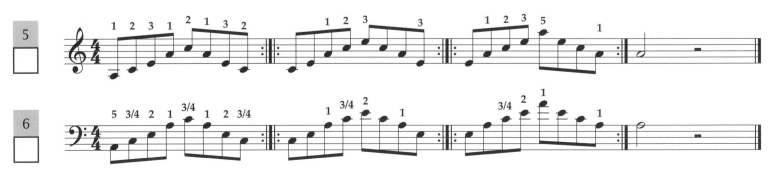

Broken chord exercises

Note: There is no A minor broken chord required for any Grade 2 exam.

Melodic minor exercises

1

Key piece   Algerian adventure

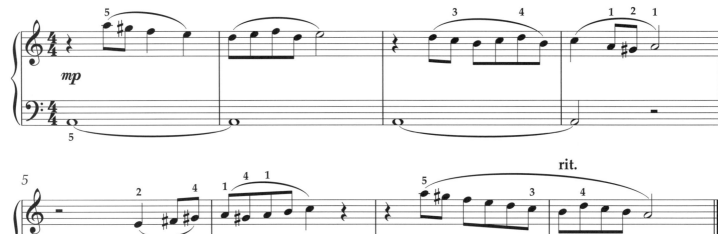

2

Have a go Using both hands, or just the right-hand line, compose or improvise an answering phrase or a short piece beginning with these notes:

3

Sight-reading

1 What is the key of this piece?

2 What is the name of the last left-hand note in bar 2?

3 How will you put character into the piece?

4 Tap the rhythm of each hand separately, then both together.

5 Try to hear the music in your head before you begin.

4

You are now ready to **say** the notes, **hear** the scale or arpeggio in your head (playing the keynote first), **think** about the fingering and then finally **play** the scale or arpeggio with confidence!

E minor

Fill in the scale:

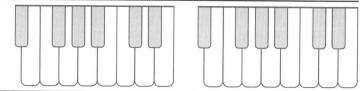

Write the key signature of E minor (treble and bass clefs): _____   _____

The relative major of E minor is: _____

Finger fitness

Harmonic minor exercises

If you play D instead of D♯, you get the **natural minor** scale.

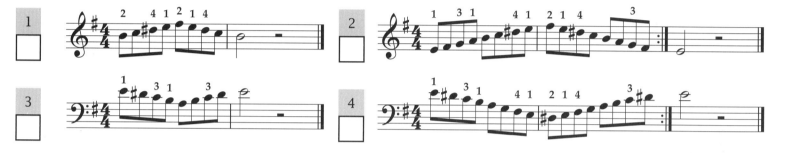

Melodic minor exercises

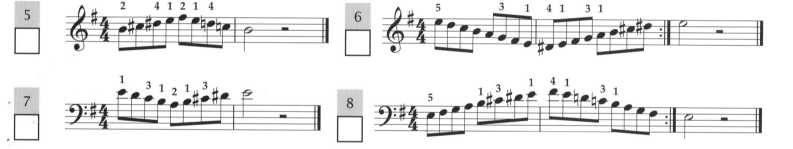

Arpeggio and broken chord exercises

Key piece   Eerie

Have a go Compose or improvise a two-bar answering phrase or a short piece beginning with these notes:

Sight-reading

1 What is the key of this piece?

2 What do you notice about the first two notes and the final two notes in the left hand?

3 Find all the F sharps.

4 How will you give the piece some character?

5 Tap the rhythm of each hand separately, then both together.

See also *Improve your sight-reading!* Piano Grade 2, Stage 6: E minor.

You are now ready to **say** the notes, **hear** the scale, arpeggio or broken chord in your head (playing the keynote first), **think** about the fingering and then finally **play** the scale and arpeggio or broken chord with confidence!

B minor

Fill in the scale:

Write the key signature of B minor (treble and bass clefs):

The relative major of B minor is: _____

Finger fitness

TOP TIP *Remember, B minor uses a different pattern in the left hand (**Pattern B**).*

Harmonic minor exercises

If you play A instead of A♯, you get the **natural minor** scale.

Arpeggio exercises

Broken chord exercises

Note: There is no B minor broken chord required for any Grade 2 exam.

Melodic minor exercises

Key piece   Ballet

Have a go Using both hands, compose or improvise an answering phrase or a short piece beginning with these notes:

Sight-reading

1 In which key is this piece? Why is there an A♯ in bar 1?

2 How many beats are there in a bar?

3 Tap the lower line with your left hand and the upper line with your right hand.

4 How will you play the piece sadly?

5 Play the first note and then try to hear the piece in your head.

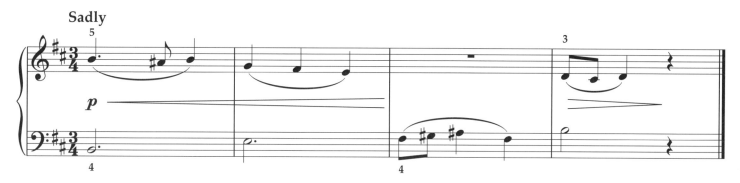

You are now ready to **say** the notes, **hear** the scale or arpeggio in your head (playing the keynote first), **think** about the fingering and then finally **play** the scale or arpeggio with confidence!

D minor

Fill in the scale:

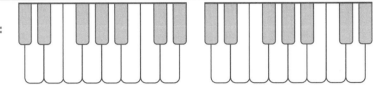

Write the key signature of D minor (treble and bass clefs): _____

The relative major of D minor is: _____

Finger fitness

> **TOP TIP** *Practise regularly with a metronome if you can, gradually increasing your speed.*

Harmonic minor exercises

If you play C instead of C♯, you get the **natural minor** scale.

Arpeggio exercises

Broken chord exercises

Melodic minor exercises

Key piece   Doubloons

Have a go Using both hands, or just the right-hand line, compose or improvise an answering phrase or a short piece beginning with these notes:

Sight-reading

1 In which key is this piece?

2 Can you spot any repeated patterns?

3 Tap the pulse and try to hear the rhythm in your head.

4 How will you give the piece a waltz-like character?

5 Play the first notes of each hand then try to hear the music in your head.

You are now ready to **say** the notes, **hear** the scale, arpeggio or broken chord in your head (playing the keynote first), **think** about the fingering and then finally **play** the scale and arpeggio or broken chord with confidence!

G minor

Fill in the scale:

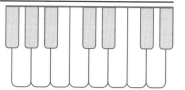

Write the key signature of G minor (treble and bass clefs): _____

The relative major of G minor is: _____

Finger fitness

Harmonic minor exercises
If you play F instead of F♯, you get the **natural minor** scale.

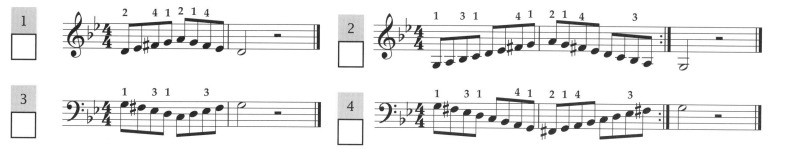

Melodic minor exercises

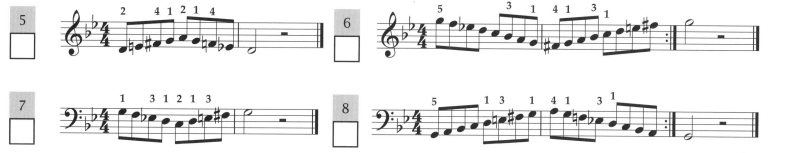

Arpeggio and broken chord exercises

Note: There is no G minor broken chord required for any Grade 2 exam.

1

Key piece   Ghoulish gigue

2

Have a go Compose or improvise a two-bar answering phrase or a short piece beginning with these notes:

3

Sight-reading

1 In which key is this piece?

2 What do you notice about the first two notes and final two notes in the left hand?

3 Find all the F sharps.

4 How will you give the piece some character?

5 Tap the rhythm of each hand separately, then both together.

See also *Improve your sight-reading!* Piano Grade 2, Stage 7: G minor.

4

You are now ready to **say** the notes, **hear** the scale or arpeggio in your head (playing the keynote first), **think** about the fingering and then finally **play** the scale or arpeggio with confidence!

Contrary motion scale studies

> **TOP TIP** *Check which contrary motion scales you need to learn for your exam.*

1

Contrary contraption Contrary motion scale study in C major

2

Eager eagles eating eels and enchiladas in the eaves Contrary motion scale study in E major

3

Grunts and growls Contrary motion scale study in G major

Chromatic scale studies

A chromatic (which literally means colourful) scale uses all the notes between any two key notes. The most common fingering uses just 1, 2 and 3 (3 always plays a black note). Chromatic passages are usually showy, so should be played smooth and fast to impress!

☐ Make a 'C' shape with thumb and 3rd finger and start by playing from F to B♭ in both hands. Make sure you keep the rest of the hand steady when you play.

☐ In the complete scales, notice there are two places where there are two white notes together – the 2nd finger is used to fill the extra white note each time.

☐ Try the chromatic study on D to see how the fingering works symmetrically. The same patterns can be used for chromatic scales starting on any note.

☐ Listen carefully for a smooth and unaccented musical line. To help achieve an even legato, imagine falling gently from the black to the white notes.

1

Double dance   Chromatic study on D

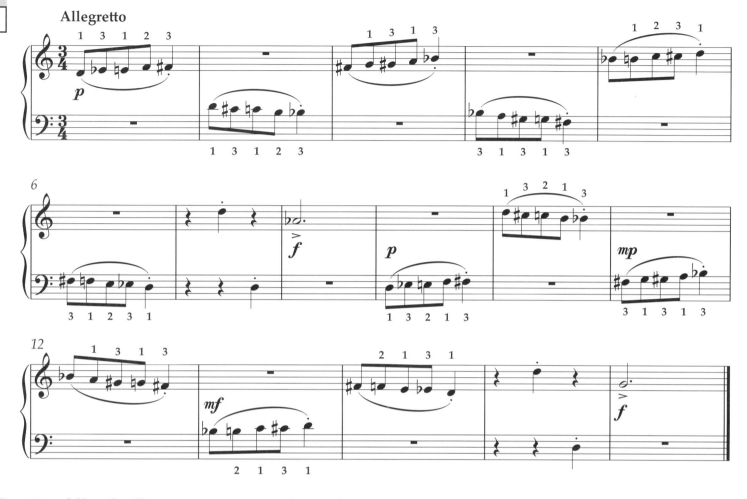

2

Bumbling bedbugs   Chromatic study on B♭

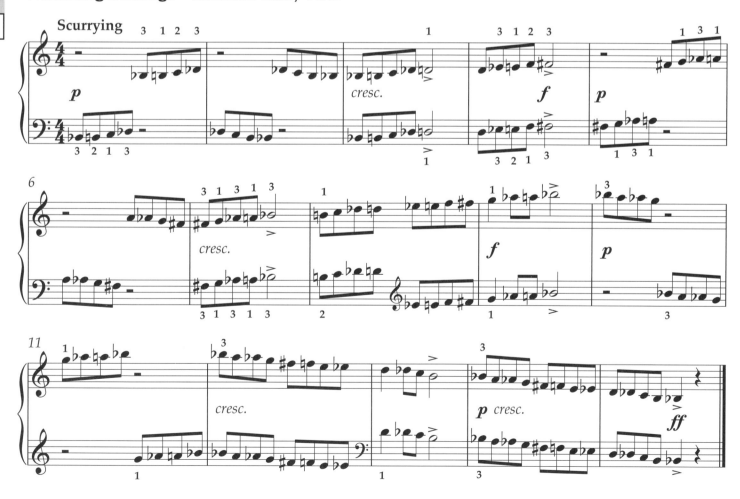

Complete Grade 2 scales

For Grade 2 exams, the minimum tempo for scales ranges from ♩ = 66–80. Try practising with a metronome, increasing the speed one notch at a time.

Tick those scales you need to learn for your exam, and then whether you should play hands separately or hands together.

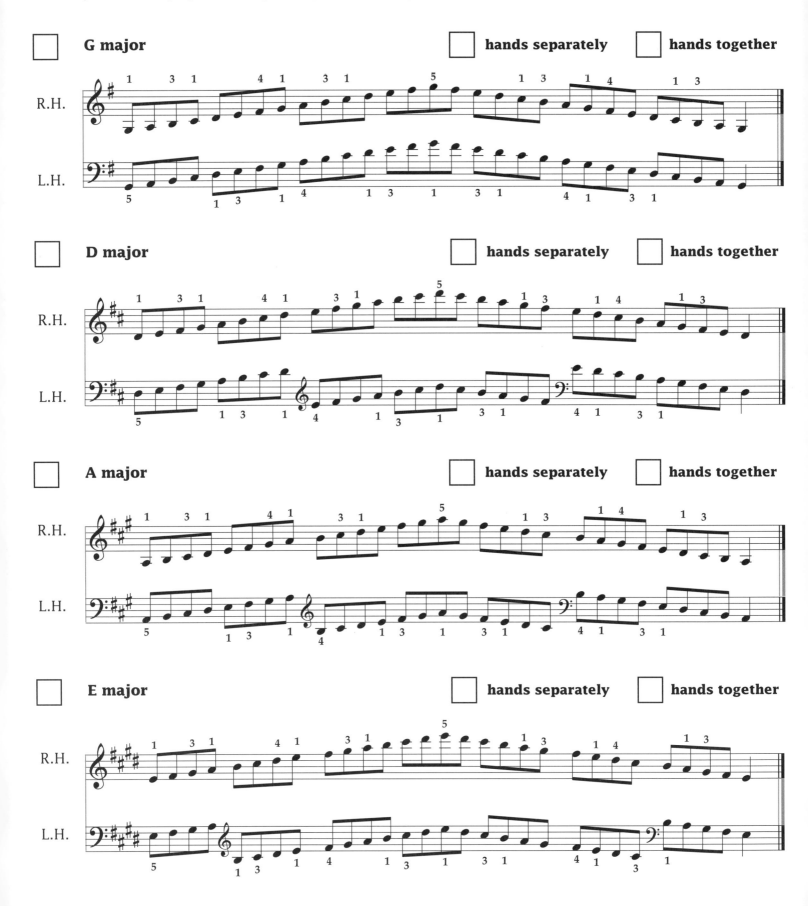

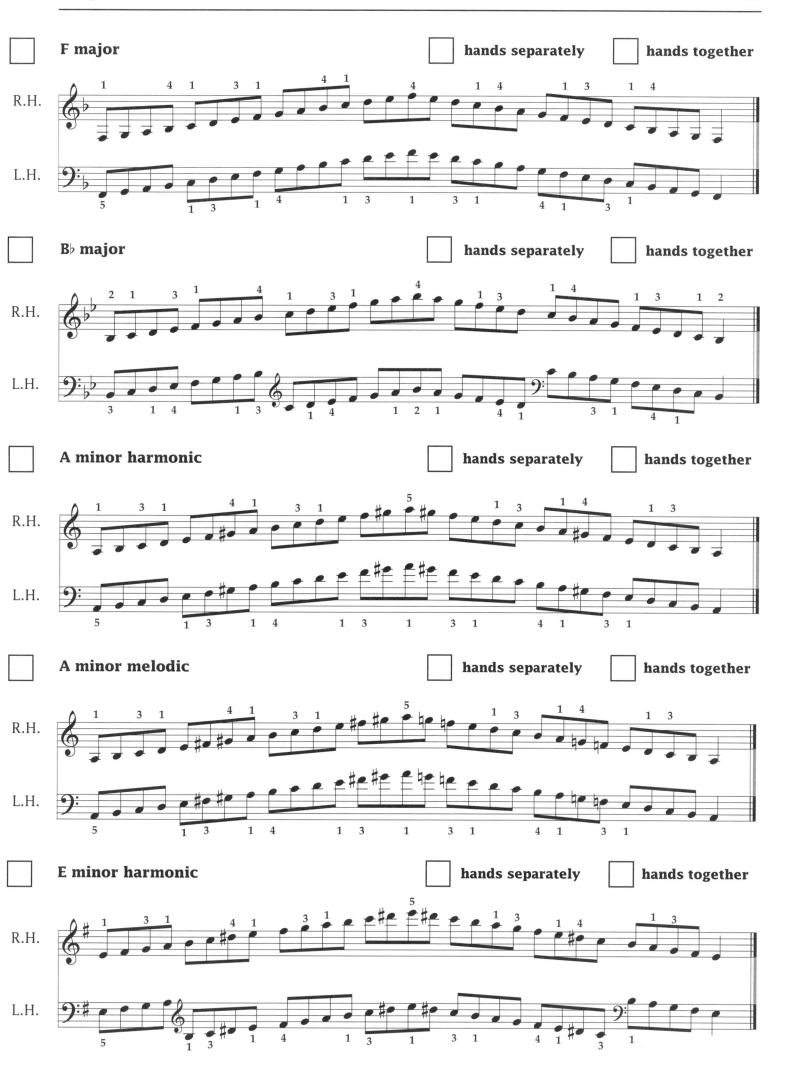

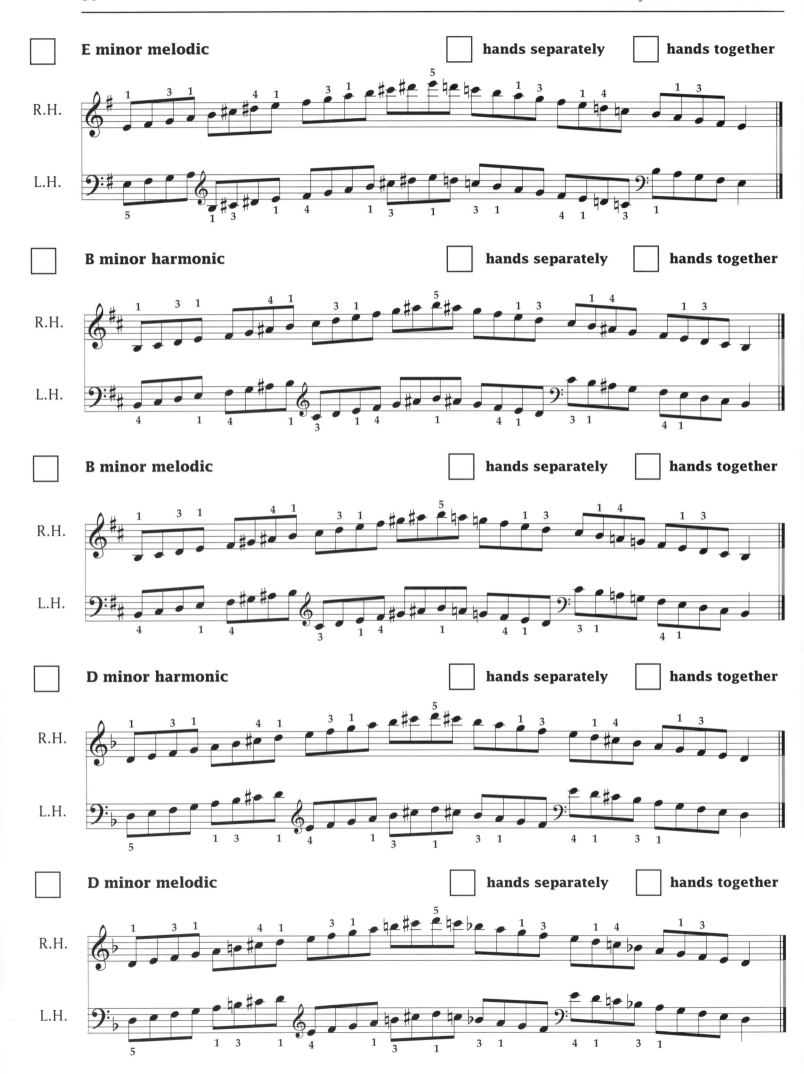

G minor harmonic

hands separately   hands together

G minor melodic

hands separately   hands together

C major in contrary motion

E major in contrary motion

G major in contrary motion

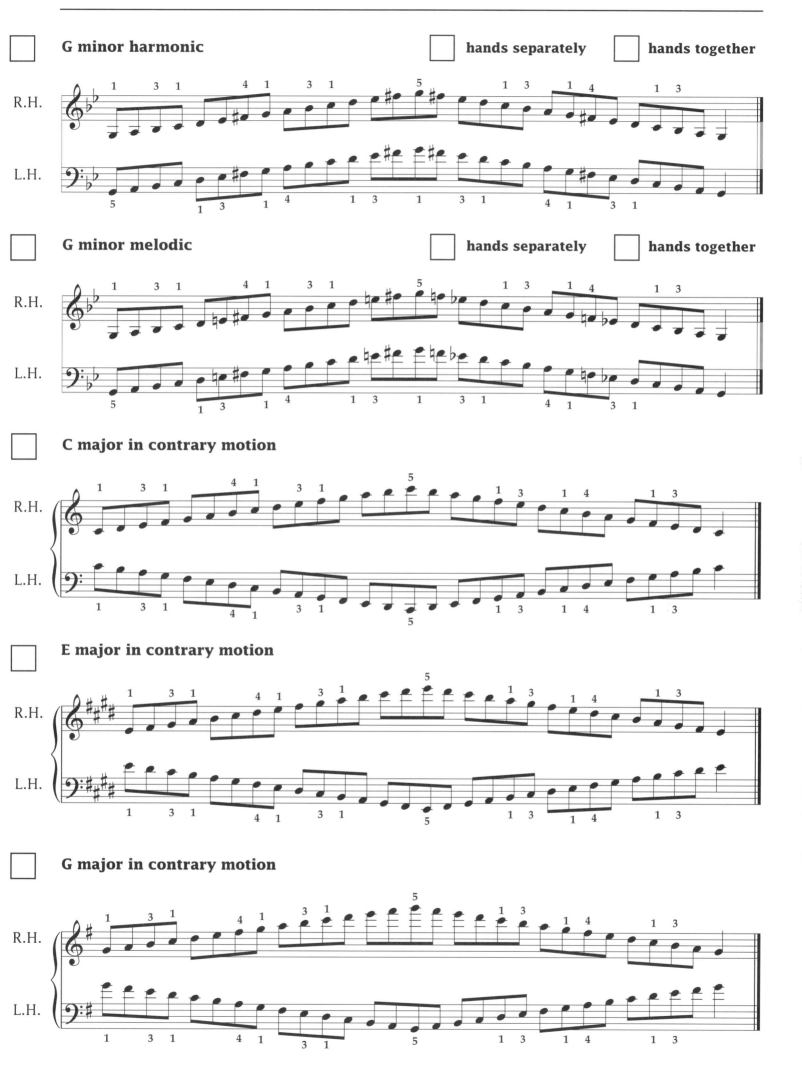

Chromatic on D 1 octave

R.H.

L.H.

Chromatic on D 2 octaves

R.H.

L.H.

Chromatic on B♭ 2 octaves

Complete Grade 2 arpeggios

For Grade 2 exams, the minimum tempo for arpeggios ranges from ♩ = 60–66. Try practising with a metronome, increasing the speed one notch at a time.

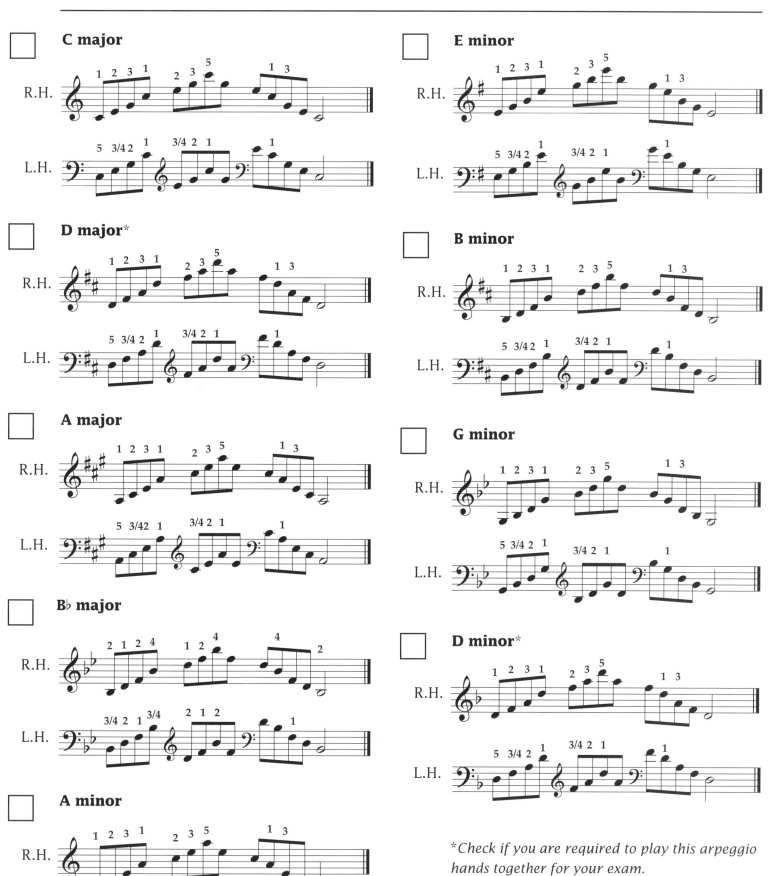

Check if you are required to play this arpeggio hands together for your exam.

Complete Grade 2 broken chords

For Grade 2 exams, the minimum tempo for broken chords is ♩ = 40. Try practising with a metronome, increasing the speed one notch at a time.

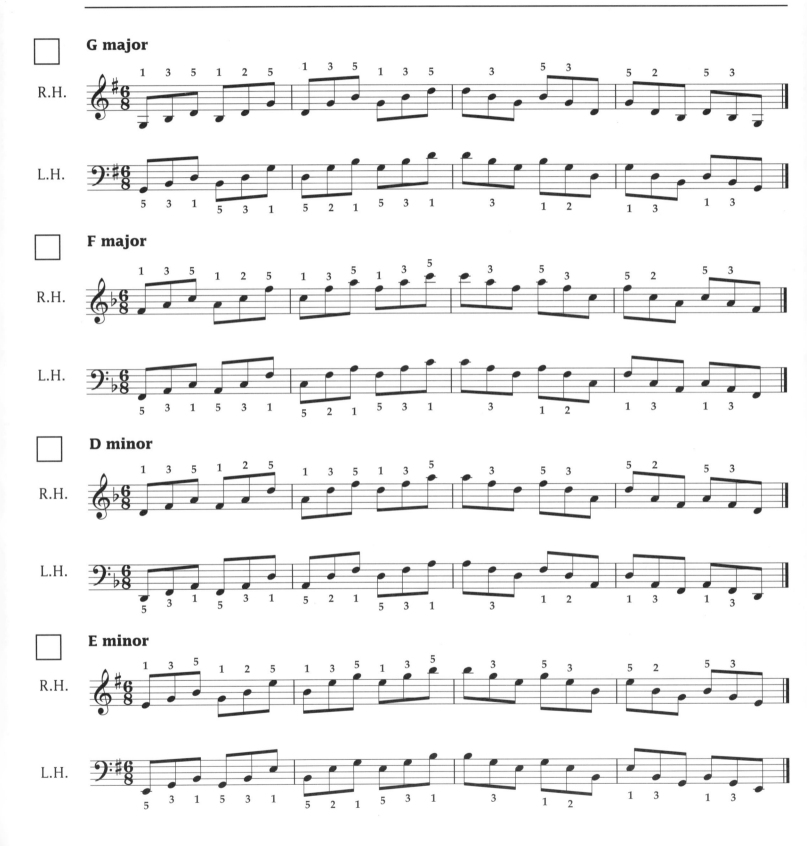

© 2020 by Faber Music Ltd
This edition first published in 2020
Bloomsbury House, 74–77 Great Russell Street, London WC1B 3DA
Music processed by Donald Thomson
Cover and page design by Elizabeth Ogden and Sue Clarke
Printed in England by Caligraving Ltd

ISBN10: 0-571-54172-0
EAN13: 978-0-571-54172-0